hawakal creative

A Matter of Degrees

Dustin Pickering

HAWAKAL PUBLISHERS

Published by: Subhra Chakraborty, on behalf of
Hawakal Publishers, 185, Kali Temple Road, Nimta,
Calcutta 700049, India.

First edition: January, 2017

Printed at: S. P. Communications , Raja Dinendra
Chandra Street, Calcutta 700009.

Contact: info@hawakal.com

Cover concept and design: Glynn Monroe Irby

Image taken from public domain:
https://pixabay.com/en/sphinx-pyramid-giza-egypt-1218603/

ISBN-13: 97893-85782-70-1
Price: $ 8.00

A Matter of Degrees

"It is not that God is the spectator and sharer of our present life, howsoever important that is; but rather that we are the reverent listeners and participants in God's action in the sacred story, the history of the Christ on earth."

Dietrich Bonhoeffer,
Life Together: The Classic Exploration of Christian Community

This collection of flash wisdom is dedicated to those who follow and surpass our age, the writers and visionaries of tomorrow … those with their heads twisted back and their hands outstretched past the gallows.

THE CLARITY OF JUSTICE AND BEAUTY

Is it odd to use economics, government, and theology to discuss aesthetics? While the latter has certainly fallen out of favor in recent decades, the first two—especially in their Marxist incarnations—are all too popular. Many might even suggest they have become mistaken for aesthetics. Some would even call for a further separation of aesthetics from economics and government, as it has become separated from theology and religion. "Aesthetic" originally meant simply "able to be perceived," but has since taken on the meaning of "concerned with beauty" or simply more broadly "concerned with whatever is artistic." The physical can certainly be perceived, but what of the metaphysical? There is physical beauty to be sure—we even have developed certain sure measurements of it with, for example, the golden mean ratio, suggesting a certain universality to at least physical beauty—but what of metaphysical beauty? And with anti-beauty movements in the arts, can we even say the aesthetic even deals with the beautiful anymore?

I myself confirm that the arts are always concerned with the beautiful, even when they are reacting against it. Meaning that whatever is concerned with the artistic is concerned with beauty. But what, then, is beauty? How does it relate to economics, government, or theology?

Aristotle argued in the Nicomachean ethics that virtue aims for *to kalon*, which can be translated as "the good" or "the beautiful." Virtue aims for the beautiful.

Keats has his urn argue in "Ode on a Grecian Urn" that "beauty is truth, truth beauty."

Elaine Scarry in *On Beauty and Being Just* points out that the beautiful is fair and that the fair is just. Thus is beauty related to justice.

The Good, the True, and the Beautiful—and the Just—are all thus seen to be of a piece. Francist Hutcheson argued that beauty was unity in variety and variety in unity. Thus, we shouldn't necessarily think of virtue, truth, or justice as singular things, but as varied things with common cores. All virtuous actions will have some similar core that all virtuous actions resemble. All true things will have some similar core that all true things have. All just actions will have some similar core that all just actions have (and, equally, unjust actions will have their own similar cores).

All of this may sound somewhat Platonic in nature: some perfect Idea in Heaven on which all perceived versions are but impure copies. However, it need not be. We can come to understand them, rather, as what are known in chaos theory as strange attractors. A strange attractor arises in a complex system through physical iterations of that same thing around an absent center that, if it were possible to reach (which it is not, or the system would collapse), would be ideal or perfect. A mundane, physical example would be rhinoceros. Each rhinoceros is an iteration of the genetically ideal rhinoceros, but necessarily always imperfect, being distinct and real. Each rhinoceros is recognizable as a rhinoceros because of all the common features they share, which can be abstracted out, but each rhinoceros is necessarily different and fails to reach that ideal. That is, rhinoceros are unified in variety and a variety of things in unity.

There is a tendency to focus on the law as something unitary, as something that comes from a single source and has a single purpose. But the best laws, the most just laws, the laws of nature itself, are hardly like that at all. The best laws are those that emerge from the interactions of people (or, with the laws of nature, things), meaning they are not handed down from some legislator, but rather are discovered. Nature has discovered the best ways of doing things (or at least, the least worst) over time, and the same is often true with humans, whether it be the laws governing society, the rules of the different arts, or the evolution of our institutions.

The best laws evolve, just like the laws of nature evolved. And there is good evidence that nature evolves toward beauty (as virtue too aims at beauty). We can see in Hutcheson's formulation that beauty is exemplified by complementary contraries, or paradoxes (not contradictions, though, which cancel each other out), such as unity in variety and variety in unity. My earlier mention of the golden mean ratio is another example, since the ratio is both rational (as a ratio) and irrational. Another example might be the way rhyming in poetry works: with an end rhyme, you both create anticipation (I know it will sound like this word) and surprise (oh! I didn't expect that word!). Paradoxes thus create complex tensions that result in—you may have guessed it!—strange attractors emerging. Indeed, strange attractors emerge at what is called "criticality," which is the borderland between order and disorder (another paradox!), and so we shouldn't be surprised to find them in all dynamic processes such as art-making.

Given the mind is a complex dynamic network process, should we be surprised that it's a critical system? And if it's a critical system, it's full of strange attractors. And if it's full of strange attractors that give rise to any sort of recognizable human nature (which would be both unified and varied), then that brain cannot be a blank slate. We are indeed built of strange attractors created by the interactions of our genes, and the interactions of our genes with our various (but not so various) environments. Such a brain is limited in what it can do and what it can learn, but only if and because it is limited does it gain the power of limits, the freedom created by rules.

In the end, all of this means that our arts are unified and varied, in cultures that are unified and varied, created and appreciated by minds that are unified and varied. Whether or not what I have written here agrees or disagrees—or both—with Dustin Pickering's musings is rather up to the reader to decide and discern. Perhaps you can perceive all three simultaneously. After all, period three implies chaos.

Troy Camplin, Ph.D
January 9, 2017

Introduction

It's odd that I use economics and government to propose an aesthetic theory. I also employ theology. The purpose is to demonstrate applications. It also is useful to give the physical world the same divisions as the breach between physical and metaphysical.

The material universe and the Heavenly universe are separate but still interdependent. If I may venture a guess (as are all things related to Beyond), human life is an open circuit channeling information into God who acts as a feedback loop. Literally, God is the Spectator prima facie who is both Source and reverberation. In it reverberation, the physical universe divides into abstract/law (the metaphysical aspect of the physical world) and the concrete/material profit. I attempt to show that the same law of bifurcation applies both to the relationship between Heaven and this existence, and certain aspects of this existence. I even imply that material forces are independent of their abstract/metaphysical cohabitants. The true spirit that anchors all being must inhabit all of life. Within these pages, the bifurcations and paradoxes become moot as does the theory of a just universe. The just universe is shown to be intellectual substance rather than reality—because it is concept and description, and does not solve the eternal question of why we exist. It is too encompassing for such a task. Only the true force of all existence can answer the Sphynx's riddle, and that is love. All else is pandering to definitions.

The basic guideline of the work is that one divides into two, and two become multiplicity. As the genders upon union reproduce and contribute to the variety of human forms, two provides the open circuit for our humanness. Multiplicity however is illusion, as we are all united in the common cause of satisfying love's wishes. This is the heart of situational ethics.

From the Wikipedia article on complementarity: "All properties of physical entities exist only in pairs, which Bohr described as complementary or conjugate pairs. Physical reality is determined and defined by manifestations of properties which are limited by trade-offs between these complementary pairs."

Abstract and material forces are complementary. From the Uncertainty Principle Wiki: "the uncertainty principle actually states a fundamental property of quantum systems…"

Throughout the work, I suggest that Heaven is the totality of all forces and existences which have originated in Absolute Nothingness. That Nothingness still exists and all things within and without it are illusory. Newton's nutshell hypothesis is substantiated by quantum physics. Matter is energy with weight. Colors, for instance, differ because of the weight of the ray. What determines the weight? This is part of the complementary theory again. Position cannot be measured if momentum is already accounted. This is why the world *appears* real. More often than not, it is position we observe because momentum is force applied to velocity. In order to sense force and velocity, we have to be in harmony with the energies and the general chaos of those energies makes this rare if not impossible. Lacan claimed that psychological equilibrium is not possible. It is this reason we feel warmth instead of the weight. After all, isn't heat the property of forces in action?

Our perspective is what changes Nature—as Einstein's relativity shows, the position of the observer is determinant—we do not have a full picture of just how "unbearable" the "lightness of being" truly is.

Dustin Pickering
January, 2017

ACKNOWLEDGEMENTS

I would like to thank Troy Camplin and Sabahudin Hadzialic for their remarks and contributions to this collection of Flash Wisdom.

My aunt Deborah, whose generosity has sustained me as an artist, is not without my gratitude.

Friends who have critiqued my musings and spurred my thinking forward are also given due consideration: Sharon Presley, Dru Watkins, the Denson family, Chuck Taylor, among others.

Patrons for my work in the arts such as Luis and Adriana Babiak-Vasquez, Kiriti Sengupta, and AJ Price are fully worthy of mention. Without their generous efforts and donations, I would not be able to continue my work and fulfill my purpose.

My partner in business Z. M. Wise has been an emotional and intellectual bulwark against my desolating moods and has been a significant part of my journey forward.

Finally, thank you to all contributors to *Harbinger Asylum* over the years. Your willingness to trust us with your work is what makes the journal great.

When I was a teen, I was caught stealing items from a shopping mall. The tally of the value of the items worsened the severity of my crime.

Crimes are categorized with their respective punishments. See, the defendant stands guilty by default. I wonder, is punishment the determinant of guilt?

Good and evil imply *a matter of degrees*. Degrees are gradients in relation to one another. Free will and universal principles are incompatible, however!

My high school theology class enticed me to think on this question. Raised Catholic, I doubt universal values because I like to build on my foundational teachings.

Yin and yang identify to balance one another, with each containing a seed of the other. A viable expression of relativity, isn't it?

Jurisprudence normally inquires into motive to judge the seriousness of a crime, or whether a crime has been committed at all.

Then, the crime is assigned a place in the hierarchy of law (Class A, Class B, Class C, etc.) based on seriousness and import of the crime. This is the secular basis of law. Justice is rooted in the how and why of a crime, and the person's situation is taken to account. Are even legal matters a matter of degrees?

Divine justice, it is said, is higher than human law[*]. What is the deciding factor in divine justice? The answer varies depending on who you ask. Some say, "Your faith will save you." Others say, "Faith without works is dead.[**]" Charity and mercy are core values in divine justice, and God asks us to be charitable and compassionate to those unfortunate. Is divine justice then an act of mercy, of permissiveness[***]? When mercy is shown, does the criminal receive less of a sentence? Does this imply that God's law is more relaxed than human law?

[*]Lex naturalis, or "natural law", consists of the principle that basic moral foundations can be discerned through natural reason, according to which a theory of human nature is developed. All positive law succumbs to its influence in theory.
[**] My critique of Lutheranism based on Scriptural verse itself. See James 2:14-26 (*New International Version*).
[***]Interrogation of Doestoevsky's "extraordinary man" theory. Was Raskolnikov merely a troubled man who went wrong? Where was his mercy?

Karma already implies the presence of a just world. If my fate is punishment for doing you wrong, then my wrong against you may be your fate.

Good and evil are arbitrary distinctions awarded to the naïve.

Sin is the absence of God, so Christians say. When we commit a sin, we move away from God and must reconcile with Him and ask for mercy*. It is universally acknowledged that kindness and compassion are key virtues.

Original sin means that our nature is fallen, that is we are separated from God by our physical existence. Does this imply that matter is a fallen state? How then does the Kingdom of Heaven lie within**?

*The sacrament of Reconciliation is such a practice.
**King James Version, Luke 17:21.

Our will is divided. Only division can create
multiplicity yet multiplicity is rooted in unity*.
For something to disperse, it must have Origin.
For our birth is a separation and separation is a
matter of degrees. One sin or two when the slate
is wiped clean?

*"While objects there are, these objects are neither unities nor
identities. No, they are multiplicities. The object-oriented
philosopher, in a desperate gambit to preserve identity, declares
that identity and unity are withdrawn. [...] Such is the phallic
logic that haunts object-oriented philosophy. [....] The
onticologist, by contrast, declares that objects have no unity or
identity. Rather, for the onticologist, objects are
pure multiplicities." (Levi Bryant, https://
larvalsubjects.wordpress.com/2012/02/10/of-withdrawal-and-
multiplicity/)

Tabula Rasa*: the world writes upon. Blank slate. As children, we are born empty of sensory perceptions. Locke speculated that sensory impressions leave their traces on us.

We are born with angel eyes and dust fills them. We are not to see our neighbor's eyes covered with dust because it is our own dust we see. Take the mote from your sight**.

*An Essay Concerning Human Understanding, John Locke: "If we will attentively consider new born children, we shall have little reason to think that they bring many ideas into the world with them" (Book One).
**King James Version, Matthew 7:5.

Mirrorscapes are embodiments of the divine. A mingling of voices.

When one looks at another and sees oneself, the Buddha[*] is the ray of light[**] between them. We see ourselves, yet know only ourselves. Experiences become our own when we live through them.

If I placed myself in my neighbor's experience, what of it? I would possess his vision and it would be my own. Even selflessness is of the Self. Therefore, even Self is selfless[***].

[*]The Five Skandhas: Form, Sensation, Perception, Mental formations, Consciousness.
[**]Reflects back to the last passage referring to Matthew 7:5.
[***]Anatta Buddhism: the doctrine that there is in humans no permanent, underlying substance that can be called the soul. Instead, the individual is compounded of five factors that are constantly changing. (*https://www.britannica.com/topic/anatta*)

They say the profit motive provides incentives and is the most efficient way to provide for the populace. Free markets, even when taxed and regulated, when left to their priorities create abundance. Abundance gravitates to where it is most desired.

This is another example of how freedom and Self, freedom of Self, can benefit the world and in essence liberate.

Abundance is best situated where it is desired. It cannot go where it is not consumed. The acknowledgement of Selfhood is the best remedy against waste.

Can we attain Selfhood in a matter of degrees? Are we separated from ourselves in parts? Perhaps seeking the Self is unifying multiplicity. Perhaps abundance is what makes the heart bold.

Principles must be deduced* from sound reasoning. This process requires trial and error as well as careful logic. What this implies for universal principles is a process of elimination. For truth to exist, falsehood must encounter it. Therefore, truth is a matter of degrees.

Are principles perhaps polar, with two extremes that protect equilibrium**? If truth sets you free, then freedom must actually be liberation from equilibrium. To be free, you must become aware you were enslaved***.

Equilibrium is the greatest slavery because it requires homeostasis****. Without disorder, a system will not know progress. Equilibrium is inertia and motion is freedom.

*Deduction, as opposed to induction, begins with argument and seeks logical proof, or data.
**Opposite ends of a magnet attract. Attraction is equated with equilibrium as it is a state of balance.
***Kierkegaard referred to "the dizziness of freedom". The possibility of acting in situations triggers immense dread. Kierkegaard posits that freedom implies the necessity of law, or a boundary, that could be transgressed. Without the freedom to transgress, no moral choices are made. The above statement reflects this paradox.
****Constancy requires guilt. Again, Original Sin and reconciliation.

Are desires fulfilled in each lifetime? Perhaps it is that we want only not to want.

Mimetic desires[*] are a matter of degrees. We achieve them in greater or lesser affront. They are no more who we are than the clothes we wear.

[*]Anthropological philosopher Rene Girard discusses mimetic desire. From Wikipedia's entry on him: "Mediation is external when the mediator of the desire is socially beyond the reach of the subject..." This is precisely what is meant by "a matter of degrees."

Perhaps it is that the cosmos are a fabric containing holes. Those holes are various roles open to fulfillment. Each identity is such a role.

Identity is not universal[*]. Some things only have identity because it is assigned to them. Without choice, no identity is assigned. Yet our roles are often fixed. The child is father of the man[**].

Even growth is merely exceeding the role[***], not transcending it.

[*]The relationship between Identity and Universals.
[**]"My Heart Leaps Up When I Behold", William Wordsworth.
[***]"…with tangible adult tasks ahead of them are now primarily concerned with what they appear to be in the eyes of others as compared with what they feel they are, and with the question of how to connect the roles and skills cultivated earlier with the occupational prototypes of the day. In their search for a new sense of continuity and sameness, adolescents have to re-fight many of the battles of earlier years, even though to do so they must artificially appoint perfectly well-meaning people to play, the roles of adversaries; and they are ever ready to install lasting idols and ideals as guardians of a final identity." (Erik Erikson, *Childhood and Society*)

A shoot breaking the shell of a seed is ecstasy. The life shivers, is born, and yearns upward while striving to keep its roots.

This process is a miracle of Nature.

Some may say, "Grow up!" I say, "I would rather grow down and keep to my roots. The soil is tender."

Famous artist H R Giger remarked that birth is a traumatic experience[*]. A human birth is like a plant birth.

The cracking of the shell is the child leaving the uterus and reaching the light. A mother's body, after having served as incubator and nurturer, becomes like the tender shoot. The man's seed is planted in her earth between the furrows. His penis is like the spade.

"Be fruitful, multiply," takes on newer meanings through this metaphor.

Growing shoots curve[**] and kick, growing wilder and larger. When the bean sprout finally breaks, a small stalk is born. From this stalk, we will see the future generation of variations.

[*]"The only way out as to wake up. I subsequently painted some of these imaginary passages (I-IX) and since then had been spared this birth trauma. But the passages became for me a symbol of growth and dissolution in ever possible stage of pleasure and pain, and they had remained with me to this day." (H R Giger, *Necronomicon English Edition*, 1991)

[**]"The breaking wave and the muscle as it contracts obey the same law. Delicate line gathers the body's total strength in a bold balance. Shall my soul meet so severe a curve, journeying on its way to form?" (Dag Hammarskjold, quoted in *The Christian Science Monitor*)

The double helix is like Jacob's Ladder. Nucleotides* hold the two strands together. The angel with whom Jacob wrestles is energy. His wrestling mimics the curvatures in the spacetime fabric.

The stone represents history, a landmark. It is the final sign of unzipping.** Permanance.

*Genetic variation is caused by the variations of bases in the nucleotides of genes (chemical alterations). The four bases are Thymine, Cytosine, Adenine, and Guanine. Base pairs are deterministic.
**Unzipping is the first step in gene replication.

History is more than a succession of events. It is also the forces that unite that succession and create each moment together. In essence, Time is a fabric that natural law sews together. Each event is catalyst for the next[*].

Cause and Effect grant the appearance of Necessary action. However, what can be known of Possibility[**]? Many forces were not employed in the making of historical Necessity. What if Franz Ferdinand had not been assassinated? Would the world wars have happened?

To know is to exist. Once we know, we have left the Garden.

[*]However, Aristotle proposes agent-causality which posits that chance is the meeting of accidental causes and that there is a thing such as a non-deterministic agent.
[**]If I may liken Possibility to recessive traits?

The Garden of Eden, wrote Jung, is symbolic of the womb*. Birth is expulsion from the Garden. Our coming into the world is learning (knowing) good and evil.

To know in the Biblical sense is also to fornicate. Is knowledge a carnal thing? Does it exist in Heaven? Was Plato wrong about the Ideal Forms?

Perhaps the Fall occurred before Adam and Eve were expelled from the Garden. After all, their punishment was meted out in the Garden itself**.

They left East and the Tree of Immortality*** is protected by a cherub with a flaming sword****, so humans may not become gods.

*Man and His Symbols.
**This reflects back to my original statement concerning guilt and punishment.
***Perhaps this is symbolic again of finality. With immortality carefully guarded, we are forbidden to know Time's opposite (Eternity). Therefore, we have no way of measuring cause and effect.
****Modernism's dictum that art is combustion?

Language makes hideous things appear bright and sensible. Imagination is a matter of degrees. Censorship does not conceal the hideous because light can shine through a straw hat. Rather, it is an attempt to dam the chaos of our inner life. It serves as subconscious* to another man's desires. Why should one man guard** another man's treasure?

*In the sense of Freudian dream imagery.
**Reflecting back to the cherub in the Garden. We were born to sin.

Meditation examines each part as being integral to the Whole, and the Whole as being unable to exist without each part*. Each part performs its expected function in harmony. The Whole is contained within the part as well.

How can a part be a degree separate from the Whole if it contains the Whole? The spirit of the laws** is a central gravitation that unites polar extremes***. Each law is part of that spirit and is created within the constraints of the whole****.

*Robert Pirsig reflects on this question in *Zen and the Art of Motorcycle Maintenance.*
**Montesquieu's seminal work, 1748.
***The law of attraction as the force of unity.
****Montesquieu proposed that a central principle must guide citizens proper.

The Sublime contains terror[*]. Terror is a disfiguration of the senses. It is a cruelty that purges the soul. It affixes by fear and annihilates distinctions. Therefore, the Sublime is an Absolute[**]. Its nature is to instill nothingness.

If Beauty is Sublime and the Sublime is sensual disfiguration, then Beauty is not a matter of proportions. It is not meted out by evenness. I cannot be forged or sculpted. Beauty then is disorder, a lack of proportion. Much in same way a great genius suffers from impairment of mind.

Loss is at the heart of appreciation. Love is fortification against loss. It affirms the loved person or object. It unifies.

Nothingness is an Absolute[***]. It lacks distinctions and is not a matter of degrees. Gradients do not apply to pure emptiness.

---

[*]"It is *recognized* that the unity and identity of an object is *nowhere to be found* in what is *given*. This recognition is greeted with horror and immediately leads to the operation of negation Freud referred to as *disavowel*." (Levi Bryant, *https://larvalsubjects.wordpress.com/2012/02/10/of-withdrawal-and-multiplicity/*)

[**]Absolute in the sense that it serves to unify forces.

[***]Nothingness unifies in the sense that it contains nothing, and does not harbor distinctions.

When my heart is torn from my chest, it is separated from my body by a matter of degrees.

If the heart of life is emptiness, then fear is the natural consequent of being alive. An empty core is a terrible thing.

The arena is full of luminous thought. These flickers are fireflies in the night of emptiness[*]. They circle haphazardly, mating with one another like thoughts learning to unite in their diversity.

The human heart is a candle and being consists of moths drawn to the flame.

Essence is benevolence. The process of life is unification. This process is assisted by intermingling, communion, and honest self-dialogues.

Although becoming One is only a nominal process[**] and not an actual project.

---

[*]In the introduction to *The Tibetan Book of the Dead* (Penguin Classics Deluxe Edition, 2005), the Dalai Lama muses on the Buddhist concept of the Mind's emptiness and luminosity. The idea is expressed in this statement: "Luminous, brilliant emptiness, is the nature of mind." (Thrangu Rinpoche, http://www.rinpoche.com/q&a.htm)

[**]Pure unity is unachievable. This harkens back to universal values and questions concerning them.

The discrepancy between real and nominal wages is the result of profiteering, the very project that provides goods efficiently for cheaper[*]. If profit is taken as unification in the sense that all economic processes circulate around it[**], this proposes that profit both separates and marginalizes[***] as well as makes amends for its own faults.

As capitalism is a self-regulating system, profit naturalizes the drives and will of the ecosystem[****].

Society is a process of continuous liberation from the things which haunt it as idiosyncrasies.

[*]Marxist economics.
[**]Unification as a central force by which all processes are governed.
[***]Marx's theory of alienation.
[****]Such is the philosophy of countries like America, where self-reliance is the core value.

The Stoics believed moral virtue is an Absolute. They asked the actor to consider right reason when approaching moral principles and to be unwavering when applying them*. They also ask that a person remain good, as purple remains purple or an emerald remains an emerald**.

If moral virtue depends on activity, then what is implied is the external force (situation) can hinder or change the moral act***. The Stoic Marcus Aurelius reiterates that a person's free will cannot be taken. Yet can we have the foresight to amend our acts to suit situation? Is a person facing death around the corner unaware to blame for his murder? So, situation conditioned to environment can rob a person of his or her freedom.

Therefore, it can also influence one's moral act. Yet no one's conscience is deterministic.

*Absolutes as unchangeable.
**Marcus Aurelius, *Meditations*.
***Activity is seen as an external form.

All moral acts belong to God. Nature is chaos[*] because there are no distinctions. Good and evil are relativities based on perceptions. What happens is the sufficient cause of Fate[**], the director of our perils and majesty.

All life is dependent on the Ultimate Cause for sustenance, and our hopes and fears reside in it.

[*]Spontaneous order theory.
[**]Acts are finalized in their existence. They are self-defining.

Perhaps freedom is a pun. In the sense that a prisoner is free when he or she is released, not before being imprisoned. For you cannot know freedom without having lost it, as the saying goes.

Earth is a finite situation, a stage* where anything can take place but Morality is anchored to just cause. What happens is necessary to the antecedent.

There are certainly fixed laws to Being, but those laws are manipulated** and revised much the same way a constitution grants the powers of amendment.

We can devise technologies ourselves that empower us to bend the laws of Nature.

*"All the world's a stage, and all the men and women merely players." *As You Like It*, Act II, Scene VII.
**In the sense of discrepancies of definition.

Love, finally, is that sustaining force we see flow through life. Much the same way blood circulates in the bloodstream, love passes from person to person with gratitude.

The soul is spherical and it is love that unites its two polar extremes, and it is love that gathers together all being into the soul. The greatness of life is in the handling of love and its abilities to travel through every degree of the matter of degrees.

Glossary

Situational Ethics: "The limitations of the ethical phenomenon to its place and time does not imply its rejection but, on the contrary, its validation. One does not use cannons to shoot sparrows." (Dietrich Bonhoeffer, *Ethics*)

Matter of Degrees: Each act varies in degrees of morality. Does the act conform to the ripeness of the situation? Are all props in their distinct places, and have they been utilized to the finest degree? Morality is dependent on "the calling", that is, answering the voice of God wholeheartedly and without reservation. Under such a definition, a full moral act is impossible because the diversity of our roles naturally leaves gaps. It is the distinct truth of God to reveal Himself in and through these gaps. Imagine all of life as a circle, and all being partakes in divinity as a fractional angle of this circle. The entire cosmos is a circle as such, and each individual is a cosmos.

CONTROVERSY

Sabahudin Hadzialic, Editor-in-chief of *Diogen*

This review is written and inspired by the excellent and inspirational book *A Matter of Degrees* by Dustin D. Pickering and it is written in controversy tone. Why? Methodologically, to be able to start a magic circle of understanding - of humans. Wherever we are and whenever we are. In the same time, *nation is the part of the history. We have just to wait for the end of the history (Sabahudin Hadzialic, 2012).*

Controversy as a matter of degrees

Ethic is the science of morality and, above all, you have to be moral to be ethical and *vice versa.*

Universal principles might be created by the energy (read: God), although if God created humans on his/her image, *eo ipso* it might be linked with free will. How? Through the will of energy.

Answer for the crime is justice. However, justice is there to avoid anarchy. Anarchy, on other hand, is freedom. From the thoughts. A matter of degrees?

God exists. God doesn't not exist. However, energy exists.

"My wrong against you may be your fate." In the same time, depending on the literacy of a kind, might be the opposite.

World is global sin. The reason for that is existence of humans as a matter of degrees.

If there is a fate, there is no will.

Innocence as a starting point of human life. Sin as ending point of innocence.

Reflections of the centuries of any existence are the part of any human being.

We might be seeking for ourselves, although we first have to understand being us as humans. Why? Being human is being part of the energy (read: God).

The truth is a matter of degrees. Of knowledge. Of myself. And others. Within the energy.

Desire is the only leading point. It feeds everything else as a matter of degrees.

We are all part of multi-identity. Identity is the part of history. History is the part of humanity. Only multi-identity exists. As a matter of degrees.

Being grown up is like understanding the environment. Although how to understand environment if you haven't been a part of the creation of that...environment. As a matter of degrees.

New birth is like a miracle. We came from the energy and we will return back to the energy. Decreasing and enlarging the energy. As a matter of degrees.

Only stone cannot be changed. Everything else does. It has been told. However, I still think that depends of the material out of which the stone has been made. As a matter of degrees.

Hypothetical questions cannot exist within the history. Why? Because, in that case history would not be a matter of degrees but only a degrees of matter. What is the knowledge? Just an understanding of an human environment. What we know is only a neutron of the energy.

I like God, but without religion. Because, religion is written by humans. Adjusted by humans. Rotten by humans. For centuries. What if Garden of Eden was really the womb? Not just symbolic.

Language and censorship came from humans. So, what after existence of humans? As a matter of degrees.

The "whole" depends on humanity. Energy does not have anything to do with that. As a matter of degrees.

Pure emptiness really cannot exist. Why? Like a death. We will be able to understand it only when we reach it.

Heart is just a pump. Within a chest. Nothing else, and more. It has been made by humans as important organ – for energy, every piece of our body is a matter of degrees.

Don't feel jealous towards those who are wearing a torch. Because, at the end the torch will burn down their hands. As a part of a path. Towards returning back into the energy. As a matter of degrees.

Capitalism cannot be a self-regulating system, because the biggest lie is that "the market will regulate everything". Why? Because, at the market people are not equal. As a matter of degrees.

Morality within one society might not be morality in another one. Ethic will judge, as a matter of degrees.

If all moral acts belong to the God, the evil ones does the same. Everything is relative.

New technologies are the way out. Only if we can use and abuse them and not vice versa.

The love is an interest. Of devotion. As a matter of degrees.

Dustin meets the following, as a matter of degrees:

Whoever would like to be a bird, it would be nice, for the beginning, to build up a nest high on a burr.

The Sun comes from the East. When you watch from the Earth.

The faith might be sometimes a sanctuary of thieves.

Time is not passing, because a time does not exist. We pass. Because we existed.

I thought that I am. While I was.

Again, without discussion we cannot move forward. And what is discussion, but a matter of degrees - of existence.